MY FIRST BOOK OF
KNOWLEDGE

Kate Petty

Illustrated by Roma Bishop

Derrydale Books
New York

This book belongs to

Design: Kit Johnson
Editor: Sue Hook

First published in 1990 by
Conran Octopus Limited
37 Shelton Street, London WC2H 9HN

© text 1990 Conran Octopus Limited
© illustration 1990 Roma Bishop

All rights reserved. No part of this book may be
reproduced, stored in a retrieval system or transmitted
in any form or by any means, electronic, electrostatic,
magnetic tape, mechanical, photocopying,
recording or otherwise without the prior permission in
writing of the publisher.

This 1990 edition published by
Derrydale Books,
distributed by Outlet Book Company, Inc.,
a Random House Company,
225 Park Avenue South, New York, New York 10003

Printed and bound in Great Britain

ISBN 0-517-05177X

87654321

Contents

Here is Your First Book of Knowledge

Are you always asking questions about everything you hear, and the people, places, and animals you see? Do you want to know more about the world around you? **My First Book of Knowledge** explains all kinds of interesting facts to you in pictures and words. You can find out how cars go, why bumble bees are furry, what lives at the bottom of the sea, and lots more. Have fun looking and finding out the answers to all your questions.

The Sun and Moon

This is Space

9 planets go around the Sun. We all live on planet Earth. Can you see it in the pictures?

Planets: 1.Mercury 2.Venus 3.Earth 4.Mars 5.Jupiter 6.Saturn 7.Ura

Did you know?..

If the Sun is as big as a beach ball ...

the Earth is as small as a pea!

The stars are really other suns, many millions of miles away.
They make patterns in the sky.

Earth is the only planet where humans live. The planets nearer the Sun are too hot. The ones further away are too cold.

Night and Day

It takes the Earth 1 year to go right around the Sun.
It spins like a top as it goes.

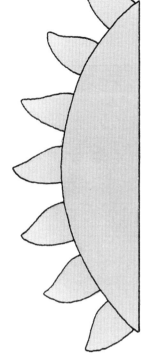

The Earth takes 24 hours to spin around once.
The side away from the Sun has night.
The side facing the Sun has day.

night

day

The Moon

The Moon is a round world of rock, with no light of its own.
It travels around the planet Earth.
Different parts of it are lit up by the Sun as it goes.

People have traveled to the Moon in a spaceship.

Planet Earth

Our beautiful world

Our world looks very beautiful from space. Can you see the swirling clouds?
You can see a lot of blue because water covers nearly two thirds of the Earth's surface.
The big pieces of land are called continents.

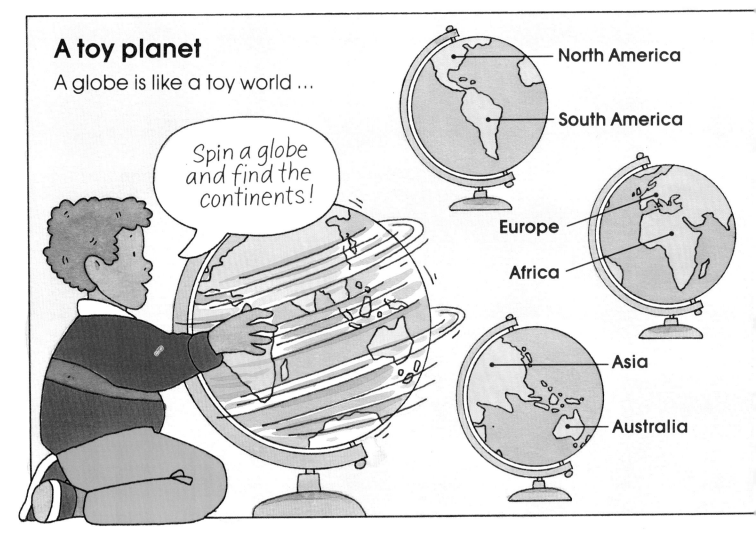

A toy planet

A globe is like a toy world ...

Spin a globe and find the continents!

North America

South America

Europe

Africa

Asia

Australia

What is the sky?

The sky is a layer of air all around our planet. We need the air to breathe and to protect us from the hot sun.

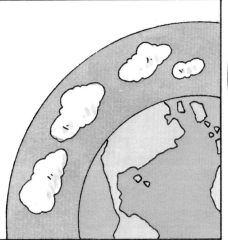

Plants and animals can live on Earth because it has air, water, and warmth.

What is the Earth made of?

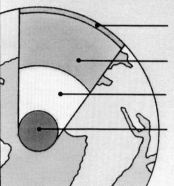

— 18 miles soil, stones and rock

— 1,800 miles boiling rock

— 1,800 miles molten metal

— an iron ball, hot as the sun!

You could never dig through to the other side of the world!

Can you find the North Pole at the top and the South Pole at the bottom?

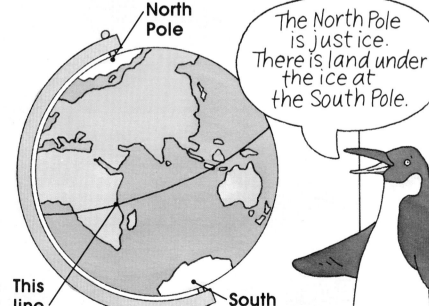

North Pole

The North Pole is just ice. There is land under the ice at the South Pole.

This line is the Equator

South Pole

Looking after our planet

Our planet is 4,600 million years old! But it is in danger. We must help look after all living things that share it with us.

The Sea

The sea is like another world.

All sorts of different creatures live there.

Plankton are the smallest sea creatures, so small you cannot see them.

Have you ever tasted sea water? It's salty!

Blue whales are the biggest creatures.

Sharks are the meanest fish. They never stop swimming all their lives.

The bottom of the sea has hills and mountains like the land. It is completely dark.

Some deep-sea fish glow in the dark!

Can you find these sea creatures in the picture?

starfish   eel   octopus   sea horse   limpet   crab

Can you think of any birds that like the sea?

The moving sea

The sea is always moving.
The wind blows it into waves.
It rises and falls twice a day at high tide and low tide.

high tide   low tide

Frozen sea

The sea is frozen into ice around the North Pole and the South Pole. (Find them on page 7.)
Icebergs are huge chunks of ice that have broken off and floated away.

Did you know?..

Only one quarter of an iceberg shows above water.

The rest is underneath.

shark

jellyfish

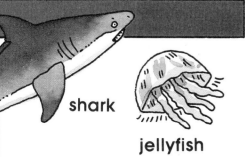

Weather

Hot and cold

Some places are nearly always
very hot. They are near the Equator.
Some places are very cold.
These places are near the North
Pole and the South Pole.

Air moves
as wind from
hot places
to cold
places.

Seasons

In other places the weather changes at
different seasons of the year.

spring

fall

summer

winter

... but we
need rain
to make things
grow!

Some
sunshine
is nice...

Snow
is frozen
rain!

Clouds

Here are some different clouds.

Cumulus	Stratus	Nimbus
means fine weather	means light rain	means stormy weather

Did you know?..

You can figure out how far away a storm is by counting the seconds between the lightning and the thunder. 1 second means a storm is nearly 2 miles away.

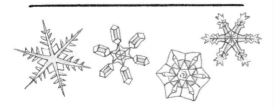

Every snow crystal is different.

Weather power

Sometimes the weather is scary!

Lightning is an electric flash traveling between the clouds and the ground. Thunder is the noise that goes with it.

Hurricanes are strong winds that travel very fast. They can uproot trees and take roofs off buildings.

Too much rain can cause floods.

Not enough can cause droughts.

Beasts and Birds

Reptiles

Reptiles have scaly bodies and they lay eggs.
This newly hatched crocodile is a reptile.

Dinosaurs were reptiles. They lived on the land, long before there were any humans.

I'm Brachiosaurus, the biggest dinosaur. I'm vegetarian.

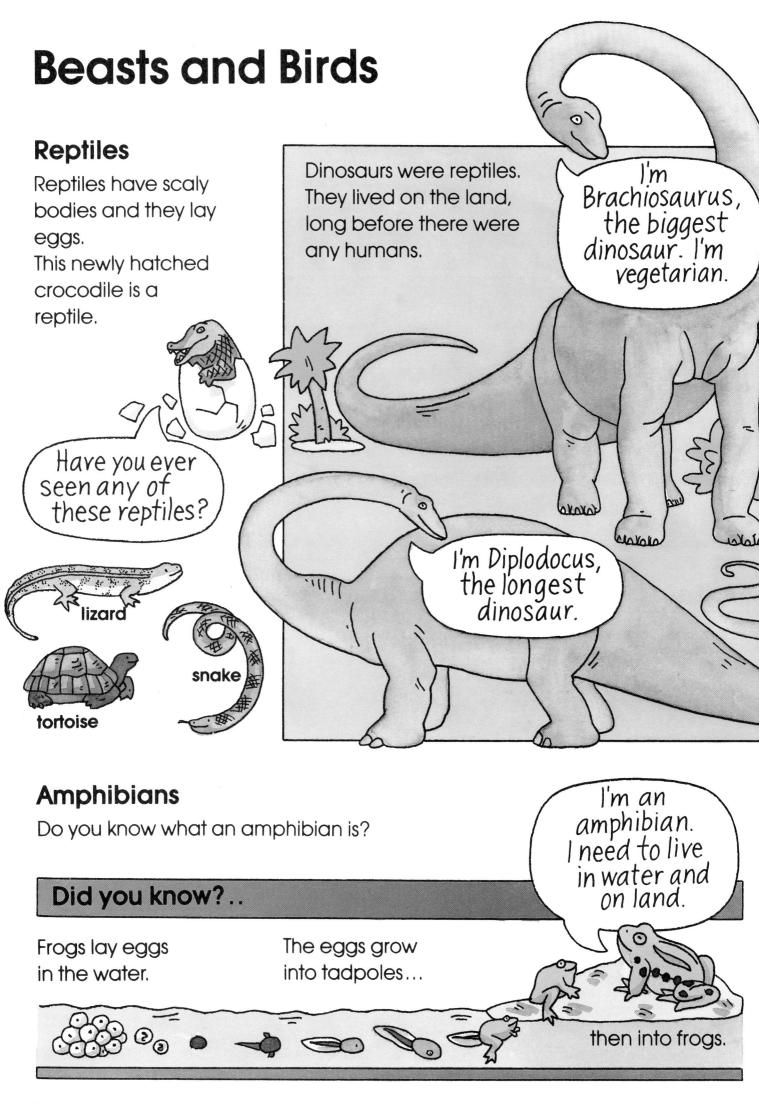

Have you ever seen any of these reptiles?

lizard

snake

tortoise

I'm Diplodocus, the longest dinosaur.

Amphibians

Do you know what an amphibian is?

I'm an amphibian. I need to live in water and on land.

Did you know?..

Frogs lay eggs in the water.

The eggs grow into tadpoles...

then into frogs.

I'm Archaeopteryx. Early birds might have been feathered dinosaurs like me.

I'm Tyrannosaurus, the biggest meat-eater ever to have lived.

Birds

All birds have feathers.

The mother bird builds a nest and lays her eggs in it.

When the babies hatch she brings them food.

Their feathers grow and they learn to fly.

thrush   duck   seagull   owl

Which of these birds have you seen?
What are they eating?

We are birds from far away. You may see us in a zoo.

parrot

flamingo   toucan   kiwi   ostrich

Kiwis like me can't fly!

Furry Friends

human

sheep

deer

giraffe

camel

gorilla

walrus

dog

hedgehog

fox

hamster

pig

mouse

bat

kangaroo

seal

I grow up in my mother's pouch.

What have I got in common with my cat?.. We are both mammals!

I am a fish. I'm not furry! Look for me on page 8.

Mammals are curious.

Mammals have hair or fur or wool or quills and warm bodies.

Mammals feed their babies on milk.

I can fly.

There are about 4,000 different mammals. Some are wild, some are pets, some are farm animals. Some are very big, some are very small.

Growing Things

How does your garden grow?

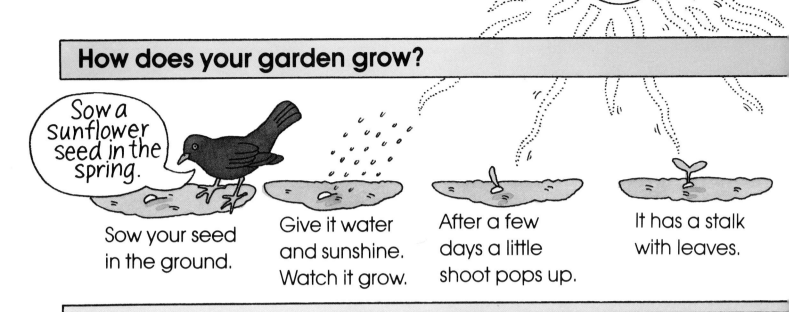

Sow a sunflower seed in the spring.

Sow your seed in the ground.

Give it water and sunshine. Watch it grow.

After a few days a little shoot pops up.

It has a stalk with leaves.

All kinds of plants

tree

farmer's crops

hedge

vegetables

bush

herbs

grass

flowers

potted plant

Which of these plants can you see growing from your window?

Different flowers come out at different times of the year.

spring summer fall

16

Bees carry pollen from flower to flower to make the seeds grow.

The little plant grows. A bud appears.

The bud opens into a sunflower!

The petals drop. The seeds fall to the ground.

Some will grow into flowers next year.

Did you know?..

Fruit tree seeds are in the fruits.

plum pit

apple seeds

cherry pit

Trees help keep us alive. They give off oxygen that we need to breathe.

Look after trees—we need them.

Trees

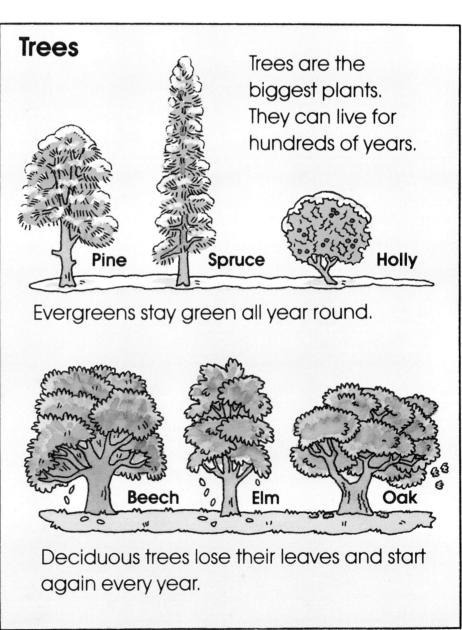

Trees are the biggest plants. They can live for hundreds of years.

Pine   **Spruce**   **Holly**

Evergreens stay green all year round.

Beech   **Elm**   **Oak**

Deciduous trees lose their leaves and start again every year.

Where Does it Come From?

Do you know what your clothes and shoes are made from?

My clothes are made from...

Wool
Wool is spun from the fleece of a sheep and knitted into a sweater.

Cotton
Cotton is spun from the fluffy seed heads of the cotton plant and woven into cloth for jeans.

Leather
Leather shoes are cut out and sewn from animal skins that have been dried and treated.

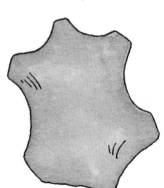

All about wood...

Wood comes from the trunks and branches of trees. Lumberjacks cut down trees.

The wood can be made into all sorts of things ...

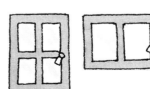

doors and windows, furniture, shelves,

This is my lunch today...

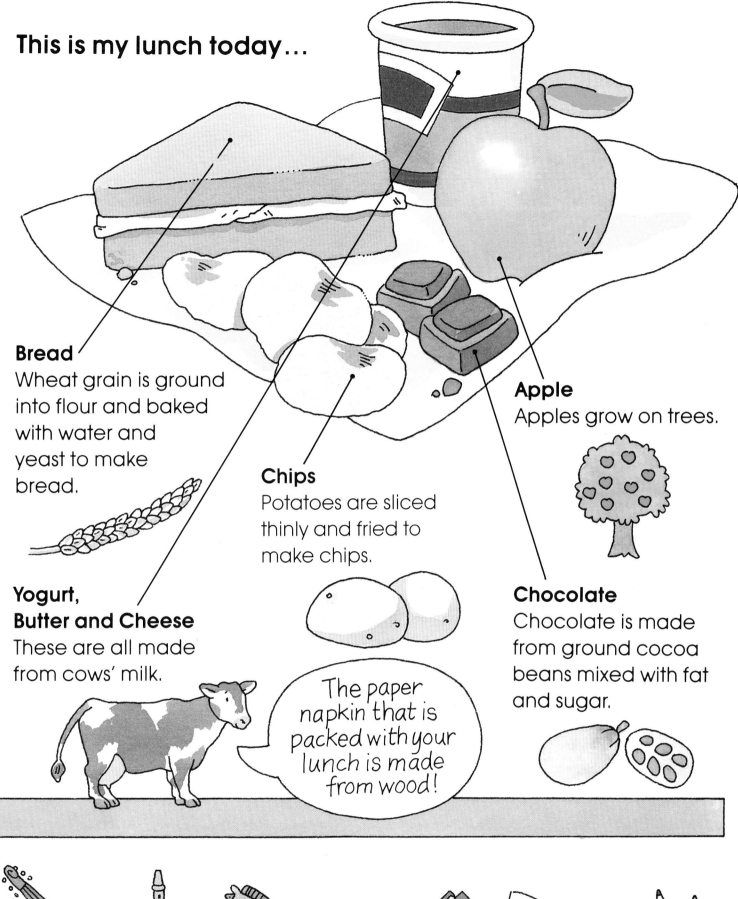

Bread
Wheat grain is ground into flour and baked with water and yeast to make bread.

Yogurt, Butter and Cheese
These are all made from cows' milk.

Chips
Potatoes are sliced thinly and fried to make chips.

The paper napkin that is packed with your lunch is made from wood!

Apple
Apples grow on trees.

Chocolate
Chocolate is made from ground cocoa beans mixed with fat and sugar.

musical instruments, toys, games, books, paper, pencils... and lots more things.

Food

Why eat?
Without food you
would die!
Food helps you grow.
It gives you energy
and keeps you healthy.
It even tastes nice!

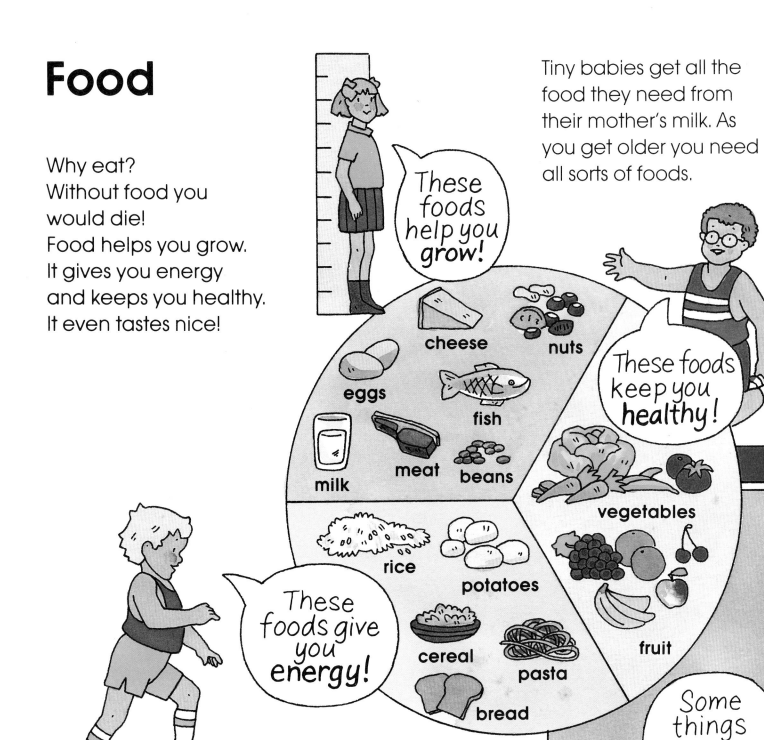

These foods help you **grow!**

Tiny babies get all the
food they need from
their mother's milk. As
you get older you need
all sorts of foods.

These foods keep you **healthy!**

cheese
nuts
eggs
fish
milk
meat
beans
vegetables
rice
potatoes
fruit
cereal
pasta
bread

These foods give you **energy!**

Some things taste nicest raw

Did you know?..

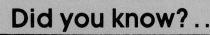

Eating carrots can
help you see better in
the dark.
Carrots are also good
for your heart.

20

Around the world

Different countries have their favorite foods...

rice
in China

curry
in India

hamburger
in USA

spaghetti
in Italy

Which foods are these children eating?

Your Body

A fantastic machine

Your body is a fantastic machine that runs all by itself on food and water and air. It hardly ever goes wrong.

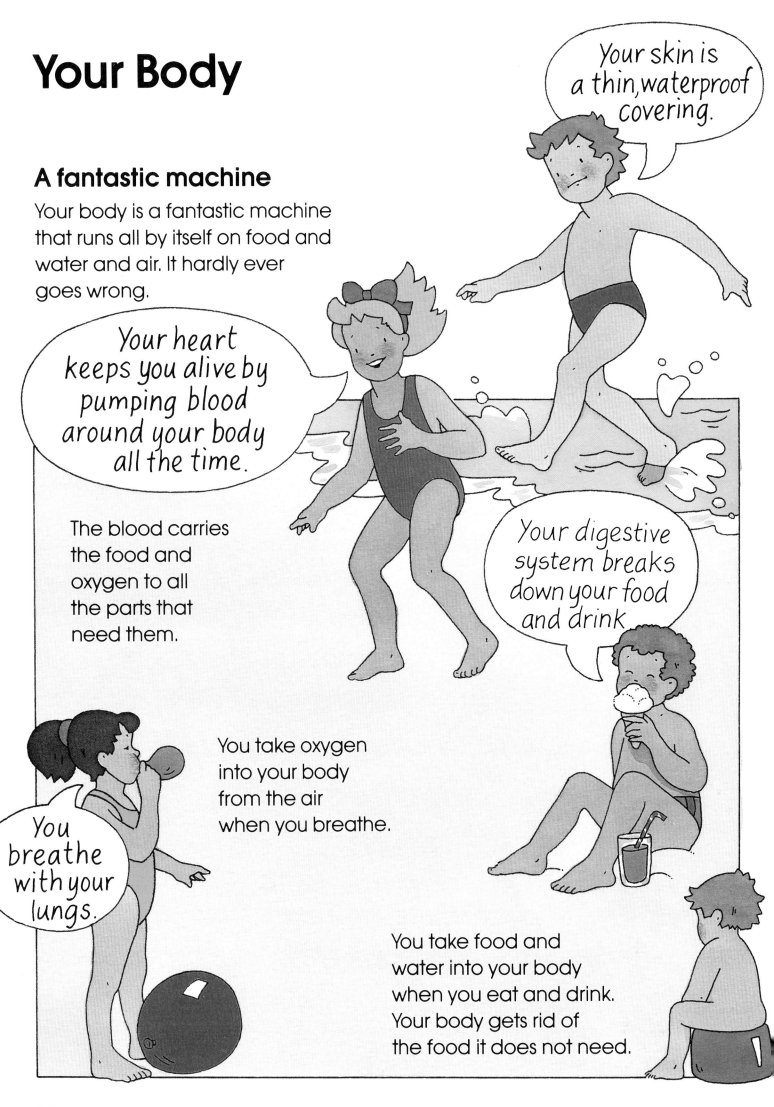

Your skin is a thin, waterproof covering.

Your heart keeps you alive by pumping blood around your body all the time.

The blood carries the food and oxygen to all the parts that need them.

Your digestive system breaks down your food and drink

You take oxygen into your body from the air when you breathe.

You breathe with your lungs.

You take food and water into your body when you eat and drink. Your body gets rid of the food it does not need.

Under your skin

These are the parts you cannot see...

Muscles

Under your skin are the muscles which help you move. They are stretchy like elastic.

Bones

You have more than 200 bones, to make you more flexible than an action doll!

Vital organs

Safe inside your skeleton are very important working parts of your body.

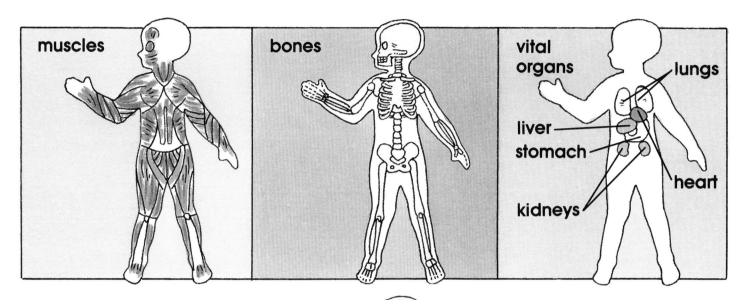

muscles

bones

vital organs — lungs, liver, stomach, heart, kidneys

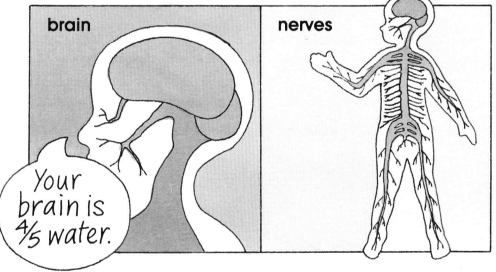

brain

Your brain is 4/5 water.

nerves

Brain

Your skull protects your brain. The brain is your control center. Messages go from your nerves to your brain all the time.

Nerves

Nerves are like wires which link your brain with all the parts of your body. Nerves know when things hurt. They tell your brain.

Did you know?..

You have five senses sending urgent messages to your brain.

smelling

Snack time!

hearing

seeing

touching

tasting

Fitness and Fun

Sports and dancing are fun and good exercise for your body.

Swimming is moving through water using different strokes.

crawl

breast stroke

Dancing is doing different steps and movements in time to music.

folk dance

ballet

Gymnastics is balancing, bending and stretching your body.

Do you do any of these things?

roll over

balance

More sports …

golf

cricket

skiing

karate

football

Do you know anyone who likes these sports?

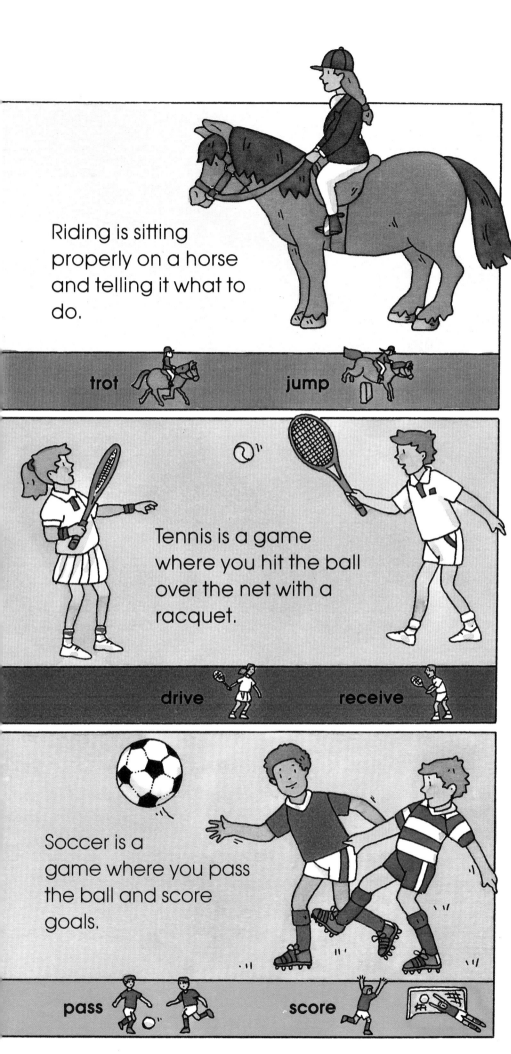

Riding is sitting properly on a horse and telling it what to do.

trot   jump

Tennis is a game where you hit the ball over the net with a racquet.

drive   receive

Soccer is a game where you pass the ball and score goals.

pass   score

People and Art

Artists

People have always liked making pictures ...

Many thousands of years ago, cavemen made pictures of animals on cave walls.

A portrait is a picture of someone. This is a portrait of my mom.

Storytellers

People have always enjoyed stories and poems ...

Long ago, before there were any books, people told each other stories.

Once upon a time there lived a fiery dragon...

When stories and poems are printed in books you can read them wherever you are.

Musicians

People have always liked making musical sounds.

You can *clap, stamp, hum, whistle, sing ...*

... or play a musical instrument like me!

People can make music together ...

in a **group**

in a **jazz band**

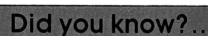

or in an **orchestra**

You can see all sorts of pictures if you go to an **Art Gallery** or **Museum**.

Did you know?..

A great composer called Mozart, who lived many years ago, started to write music when he was only 5 years old!

Visiting the Past

Do you sometimes wish you could travel back in time and see how other people used to live?

The Ancient Egyptians

Let's travel back 5,000 years to visit the Ancient Egyptians far away in sunny Egypt.

It took 300,000 of us 20 years to build the Great Pyramid!

We built pyramids like these, where we buried our kings with all their treasures.

When the kings died their bodies were wrapped in special bandages to preserve them.

The Egyptians used picture writing, called hieroglyphs.

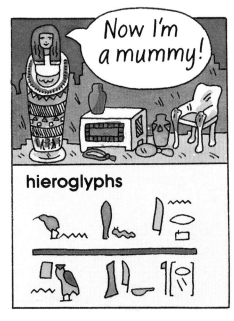

Now I'm a mummy!

hieroglyphs

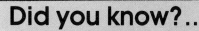

Did you know?..

Cleopatra was an Egyptian queen...

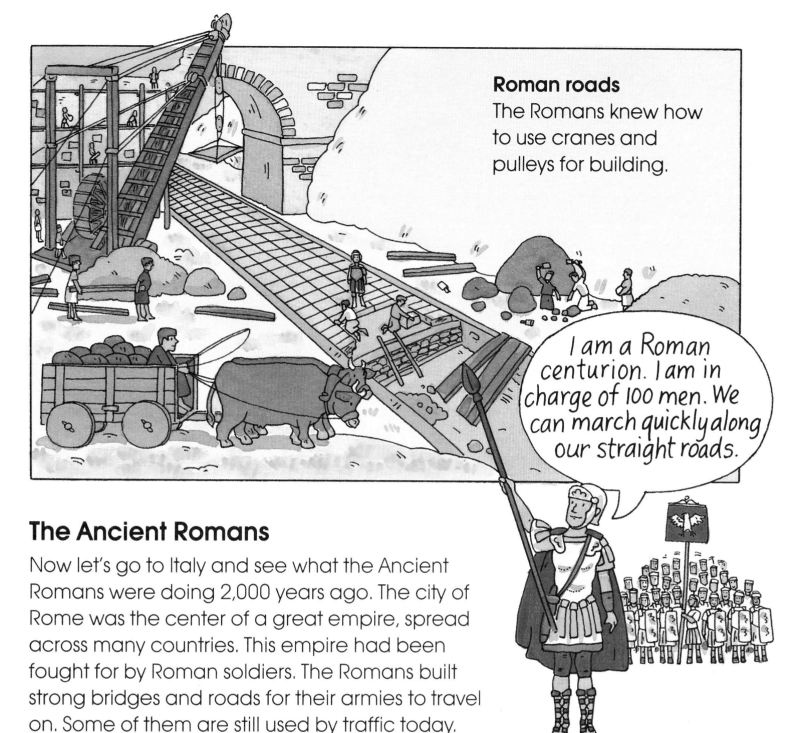

Roman roads

The Romans knew how to use cranes and pulleys for building.

I am a Roman centurion. I am in charge of 100 men. We can march quickly along our straight roads.

The Ancient Romans

Now let's go to Italy and see what the Ancient Romans were doing 2,000 years ago. The city of Rome was the center of a great empire, spread across many countries. This empire had been fought for by Roman soldiers. The Romans built strong bridges and roads for their armies to travel on. Some of them are still used by traffic today.

who fell in love with Mark Antony, a Roman general.

I'm looking forward to a nice warm bath.

The Romans went to public baths to keep clean. They met their friends there too.

Exciting Places

The world is full of exciting faraway places that you might visit one day.

Here are some postcards from each continent in the world.

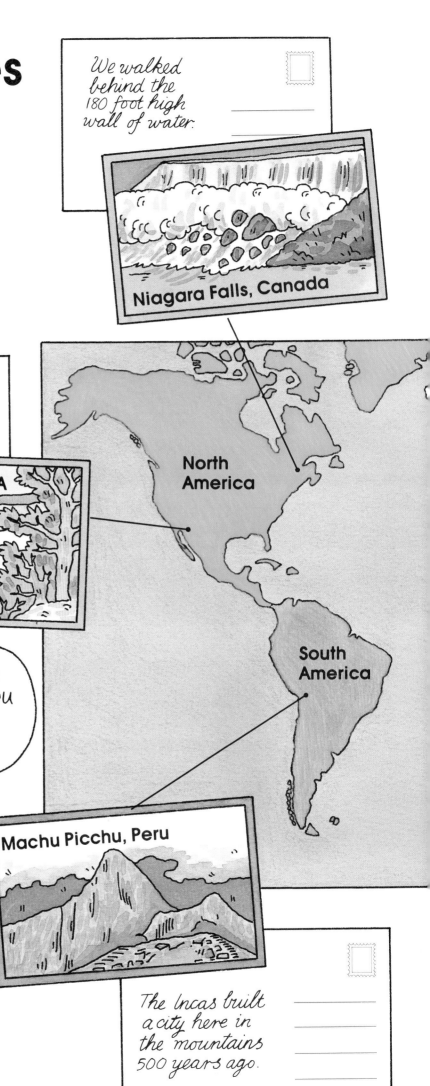

We walked behind the 180 foot high wall of water.

Niagara Falls, Canada

We rode nearly a mile to the bottom on ponies.

Grand Canyon, USA

North America

South America

Where in the world would you like to go on holiday?

Machu Picchu, Peru

The Incas built a city here in the mountains 500 years ago.

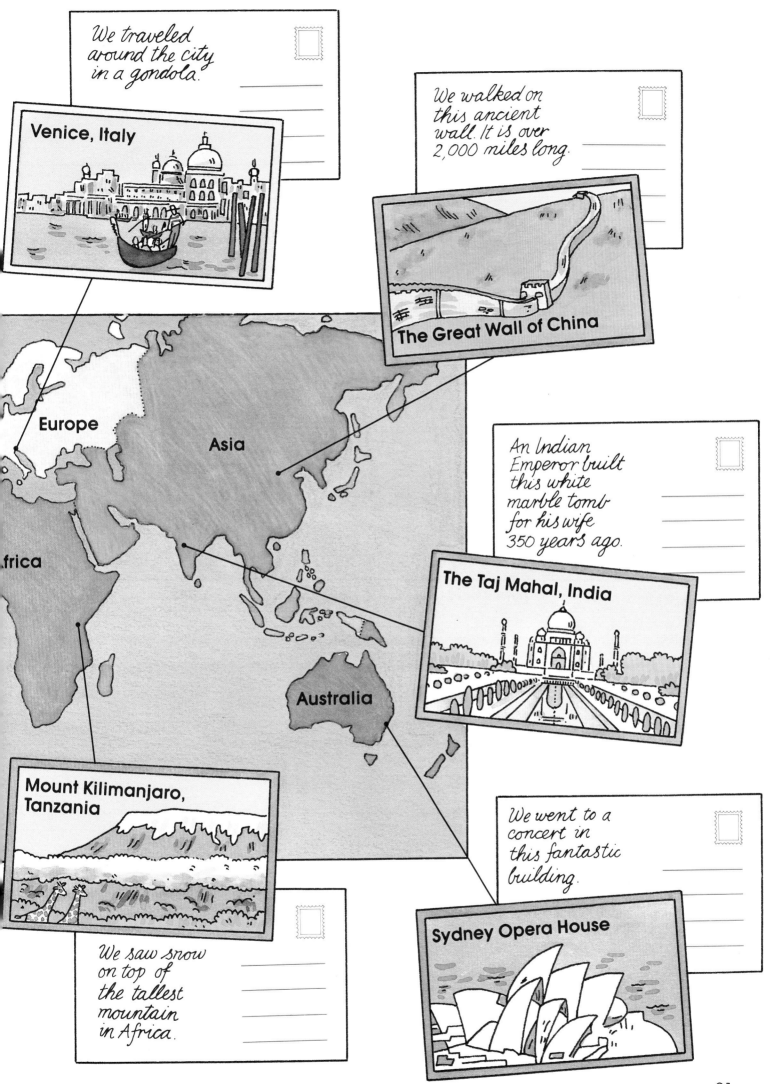

We traveled around the city in a gondola.

Venice, Italy

We walked on this ancient wall. It is over 2,000 miles long.

The Great Wall of China

An Indian Emperor built this white marble tomb for his wife 350 years ago.

The Taj Mahal, India

Europe

Asia

Africa

Australia

Mount Kilimanjaro, Tanzania

We saw snow on top of the tallest mountain in Africa.

We went to a concert in this fantastic building.

Sydney Opera House

31

The Working Day

Here are lots of people working hard at their jobs. Some of them have to work at night when you are asleep!

What work would you like to do when you grow up?

	an office worker	a nurse
wee hours		
early morning		
mid morning		
midday		
early afternoon		
mid afternoon		
early evening		
late evening		
midnight		

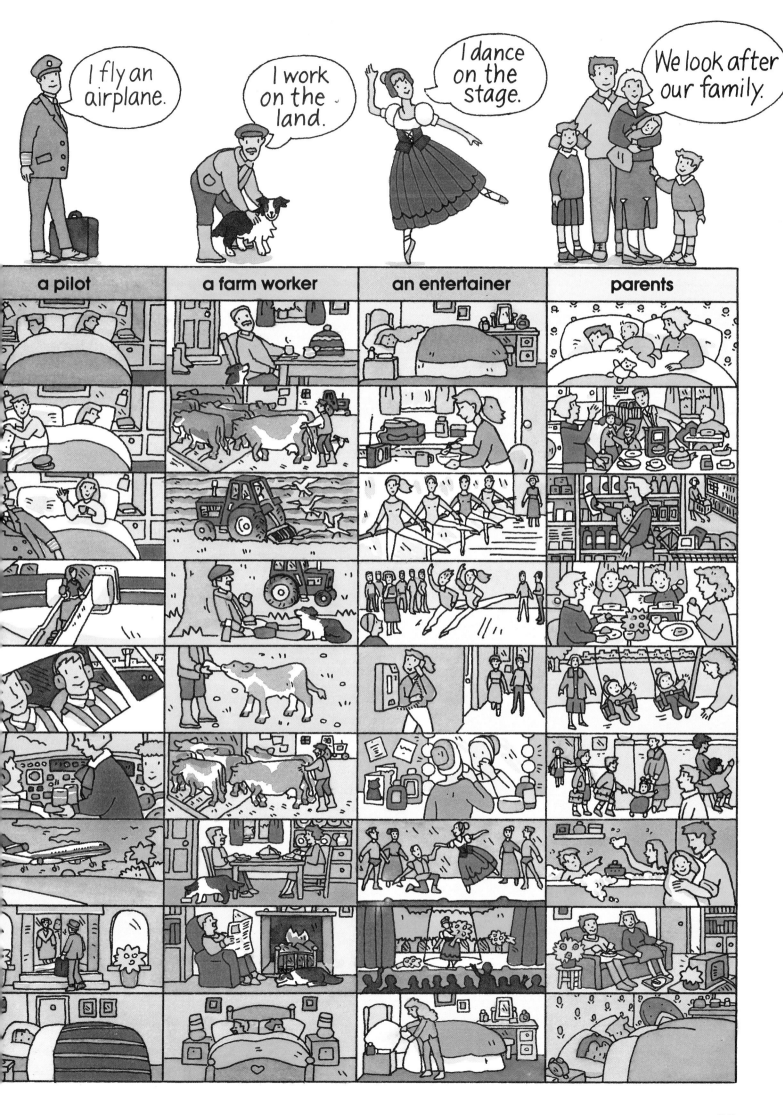

Stage and Screen

At the circus

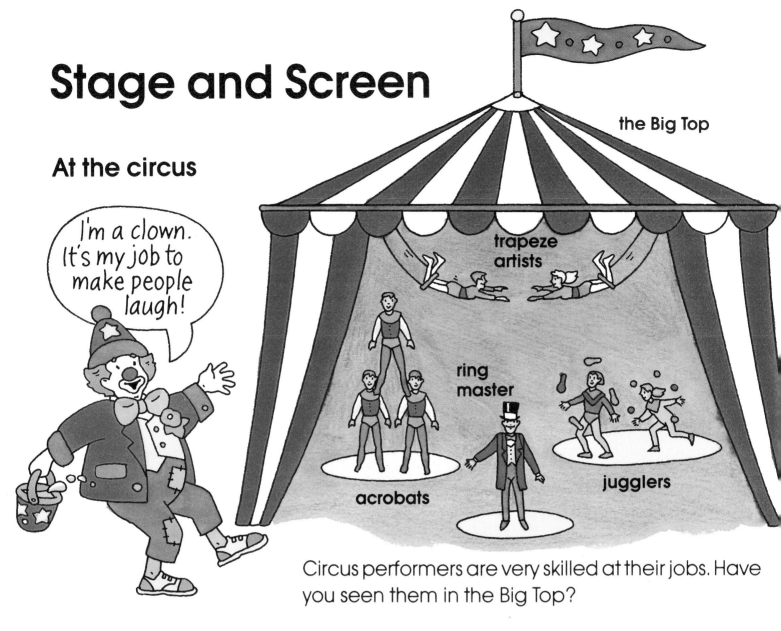

I'm a clown. It's my job to make people laugh!

the Big Top

trapeze artists

ring master

acrobats

jugglers

Circus performers are very skilled at their jobs. Have you seen them in the Big Top?

At the theater

Actors wear make-up so that people at the back of the audience can see their faces. Can you see all the people working behind the scenes?

wings

curtain

We are the audience!

We are the actors.

lights

scenery

props

stage

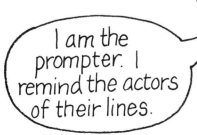

I am the prompter. I remind the actors of their lines.

Each cartoon frame (picture) is a little bit different from the one before. The pictures follow one another so quickly that the characters seem to move.

... It's magic!

On television

In a tv studio a cameraperson takes moving pictures that are transmitted to your tv screen at home. A tv director tells the cameraperson which pictures to take. An editor cuts out the pictures which are not needed before the program is transmitted.

35

What Makes It Go?

cycling   running   riding   walking   roller skating

We can move without fuel!

How do cars go?

The motor is driven by tiny explosions when the gasoline is mixed with hot air.

Cars use gasoline

The explosions fire the **pistons**...

the pistons turn the **crankshaft**...

the crankshaft turns the **driveshaft**...

the driveshaft turns the **gears** on the **axle**...

... and the wheels go around! Brrrm Brrrm!

How do diesel trains go?

A diesel engine makes electricity to power the motor that turns the wheels.

How do airplanes and helicopters stay in the air?

An airplane's wings are shaped so that the air lifts them up.

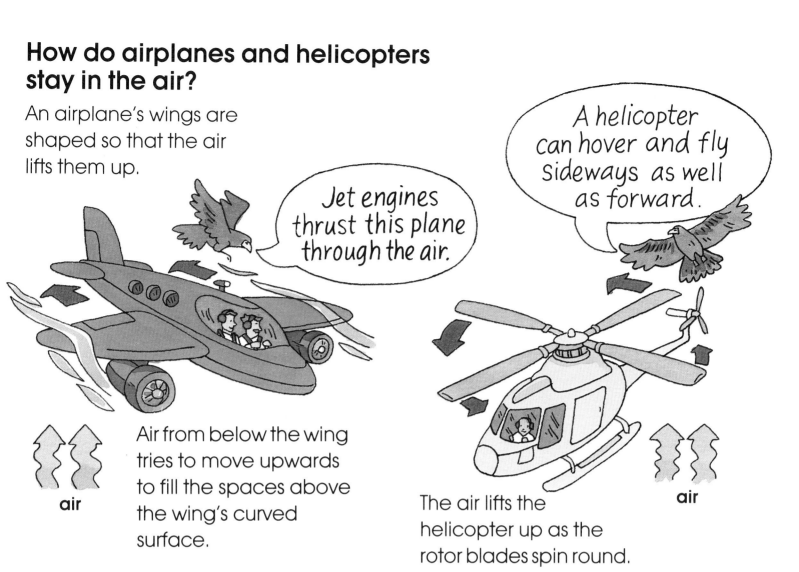

Air from below the wing tries to move upwards to fill the spaces above the wing's curved surface.

air

The air lifts the helicopter up as the rotor blades spin round.

air

How do boats go?

This boat is driven along by a propeller under the water.
The propeller is turned by a diesel engine.

propellers

propeller

Amazing Technology

Try this one!
Knock once for
'yes'...

... and
twice for 'no.'

Invisible power

Lots of things work with forces that we can't see.
Sound, light, heat and radio waves are invisible, but
like water they all flow. Their flow can be blocked
and unblocked to make codes and carry
messages.

I am a robot!
The computer inside me
stores instructions that
tell me how to move.

Computers

Computers store messages in code.
You decode the message and it
reappears instantly for you as a
picture or sound.

Recording a video

When you record a film the pictures
and sounds are coded and stored
on tape for you to watch later.

Satellites

bounce

The computer on this satellite helps bounce coded messages from one side of the world to the other.

bounce

Hello, dear! I'm phoning you all the way from England.

Hello, Grandma! You sound as if you are just next door.

Mission control

Space mission control guides astronauts safely back to Earth.

We couldn't have made our journey without the help of modern technology.

Fascinating Facts

You have about 100,000 hairs on your head!

I'm a reticulated python, from Asia. I'm 30 feet long and I'm the longest snake in the world.

We are The Beatles, the most successful pop group ever. We've sold over 1,000 million tapes and records.

The Eiffel Tower is nearly 1,000 feet high. It is the most famous building in France.

This little space probe, Voyager, has sent us exciting close-up pictures of other distant planets.

A coral reef is made from skeletons of many tiny sea creatures called coral polyps.

The tiniest t set you can bu is only 6 inche high

200 million years ago there was just one giant continent, called Pangaea.

I can carry the space shuttle on my back.

The world's biggest plane is the Russian Antonove An-225 Mriya. It weighs nearly 600 tons.

400 years ago Sir Walter Raleigh brought the first potato to Europe from America.

It's over 360 feet high!

The tallest tree in the world is the Giant Redwood in California.

I'm a cheetah, from Africa. I'm the fastest animal on Earth. I can run as fast as a sports car.

Champion boxers earn more in a minute than anyone else.

I'm Vincent Van Gogh. My paintings are some of the most famous in the world.